W9-DIY-497

¡Barcos!
¡Barcos!
¡Barcos!

Boats! Boats! Boats!

Jo Cleland

Rourke

Publishing LLC
Vero Beach, Florida 32964

*Este libro se puede cantar al son de
la música de "Row, Row, Row Your Boat".*

*This book can be sung to the tune of
"Row, Row, Row Your Boat."*

www.rourkepublishing.com

PHOTO CREDITS: © Janice Richard, © Michael Walker, © Keith Binns: Cover; © Janice Richard: Title Page; © Kirill Zdorov: page 3; © Brian Raisbeck: page 4, 5; © Glenda Powers: page 6, 7; © Frank van Haalen: page 8, 9, 16, 17, 22, 23; © Matthew Ragen: page 10, 11, 23; Daniel MAR: page 12, 13; © Javier Fontanella: page 14, 15; © Ron Hohehaus: page 18, 19, 23; © Martin Kucera: page 20, 21; © Michael Walker: page 22;

Editor: Kelli Hicks

Cover and Interior designed by: Renee Brady

Spanish Editorial Services by Cambridge BrickHouse, Inc.   www.cambridgebh.com

Library of Congress Cataloging-in-Publication Data

Cleland, Joann.
  Boats! boats! boats! / Jo Cleland.
     p. cm. -- (My first discovery library)
  Includes index.
  ISBN 978-1-60472-526-1
  1. Boats and boating --Juvenile literature.
  VM150 .C582 2009
  623.82 22
                              2008027361

Printed in the USA

CG/CG

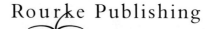

Rourke Publishing

www.rourkepublishing.com – rourke@rourkepublishing.com
Post Office Box 3328, Vero Beach, FL 32964

Mira la bella lancha.
El agua lanzará.

See the motorboat.
Watch the water spray.

3

El velero se desliza.

See the sailboat glide along.

4

Se mecerá y bajará.

Watch it dip and sway.

Mira el bote de remo.

See the rowboat go.

El lago cruzará.

Watch it cross the lake.

7

Contra el barco
de pescar,
olas grandes
romperán.

8

See the workers'
fishing boat.
Watch the big
waves break.

9

La balsa salvavidas
flotando se irá.

See the lifeboat bob.
Watch it float away.

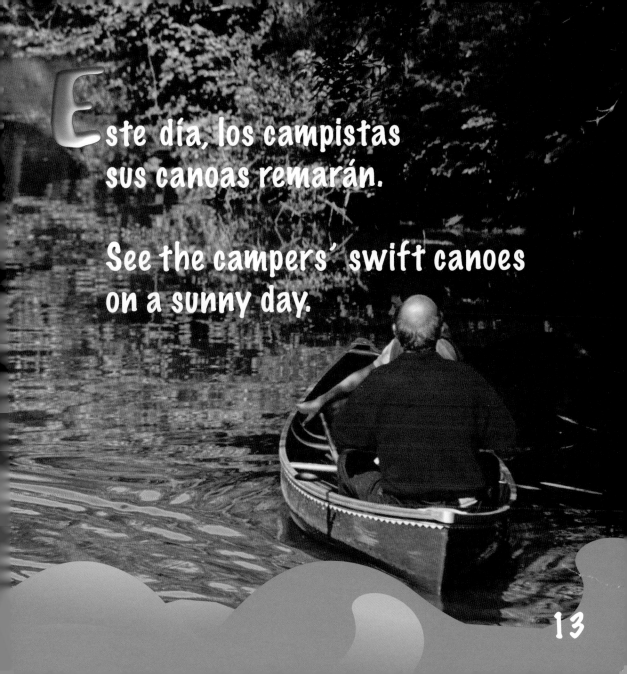

Este día, los campistas
sus canoas remarán.

See the campers' swift canoes
on a sunny day.

13

Mira el remolcador.
Lo escucho traquetear.

Hear the tugboat chug.
Watch it work today.

La sirena suena y suena.

Hear the foghorn honk and honk.

"¡Ya déjenme pasar!"

"Get out of my way!"

17

Mi bote está en la playa.

See my beach boat.

18

Es hora de jugar.

Hear me splash and play.

19

Con mi bote de juguete
gozo mucho. ¡Hurra! ¡Hurra!

See the toy boat in my bath.
It's lots of fun! Hooray!

Glosario / Glossary

balsa salvavidas: Una balsa salvavidas es un bote pequeño que se mantiene en un barco grande para que la gente lo use en caso de emergencia. Algunas balsas salvavidas pueden transportar a 50 personas.
lifeboat (LIFE-boht): A lifeboat is a small boat kept on a big ship for people to use in an emergency. Some lifeboats can carry 50 people.

lago: Un lago es una masa de agua rodeada por tierra. La mayoría de los lagos tienen agua dulce. Los lagos son más grandes y más profundos que los estanques.
lake (LAKE): A lake is a big body of water with land around it. Most lakes are freshwater. Lakes are bigger and deeper than ponds.

olas: Las olas son ondas de agua causadas por los barcos en movimiento. A los delfines les gusta nadar en las olas de los barcos.
waves (WAYVZ): Waves are the curls of water made by moving boats. Dolphins like to swim in boat waves.

playa: La playa es la tierra arenosa a la orilla de una masa de agua. Las playas se encuentran a la orilla de los océanos, los ríos y los lagos.
beach (BEECH): A beach is the sandy land next to a body of water. Beaches can be found by oceans, rivers, and lakes.

sirena: Una sirena es la bocina de un barco. Se usa en las noches de neblina para mantener los barcos fuera de peligro. El sonido de una sirena es un sonido profundo y bajo.
foghorn (FOG-horn): A foghorn is a boat's horn. It is used on foggy nights to keep boats safe. The sound of a foghorn is deep and low.

Índice / Index

Lecturas adicionales / Further Reading

Armentrout, David and Patricia. *Ships.* Rourke, 2004.
Barton, Byron. *Boats.* HarperCollins, 1986.
Pallotta, Jerry. *The Boat Alphabet Book.* Charlesbridge, 1998.

Sitios web / Websites

http://pbskids.org/zoom/activities/sci/boatsafloat.html
http://www.gamerevolt.com/game/10946/Mini-Boat-Race.html
http://www.boatingsidekicks.com/besafe.htm

Sobre la autora / About the Author

A Jo Cleland le encanta escribir libros, componer canciones y crear juegos. A ella le encanta leer, cantar y jugar con los niños.

Jo Cleland loves to write books, compose songs, and make games. She loves to read, sing, and play games with children.

24